50 Italian Restaurant Recipes for Home

By: Kelly Johnson

Table of Contents

- Farro Salad
- Grilled Octopus
- Ricotta Cheesecake
- Fagottini di Pasta
- Insalata di Mare
- Polenta with Mushrooms
- Frittelle di Mele
- Tagliatelle al Tartufo
- Zucchini Noodles with Pesto
- Prosciutto e Melone
- Sgombro Marinato
- Crespelle alla Fiorentina
- Baked Ziti
- Limoncello Torte
- Affogato

Spaghetti Aglio e Olio

Ingredients

- **400g (14 oz)** spaghetti
- **4-6 cloves** garlic, thinly sliced
- **½ cup** extra virgin olive oil
- **1 tsp** red pepper flakes (adjust to taste)
- **Salt**, to taste
- **Fresh parsley**, chopped (about ¼ cup)
- **Grated Parmesan cheese** (optional)
- **Zest of 1 lemon** (optional)

Instructions

1. **Cook the Pasta**:
   - Bring a large pot of salted water to a boil. Add the spaghetti and cook according to package instructions until al dente. Reserve about 1 cup of pasta water, then drain the pasta.
2. **Prepare the Sauce**:
   - In a large skillet, heat the olive oil over medium heat. Add the sliced garlic and red pepper flakes. Sauté until the garlic is golden and fragrant, about 2-3 minutes. Be careful not to burn the garlic.
3. **Combine**:
   - Add the drained spaghetti to the skillet. Toss to coat the pasta in the oil and garlic mixture. If the pasta seems dry, add some reserved pasta water a little at a time until you reach your desired consistency.
4. **Season**:
   - Stir in the chopped parsley, and season with salt to taste. If using, add lemon zest for extra brightness.
5. **Serve**:
   - Divide the pasta among plates and sprinkle with grated Parmesan cheese if desired. Enjoy!

Tips

- For extra flavor, consider adding a squeeze of lemon juice or some toasted breadcrumbs for crunch.
- Customize the spice level by adjusting the amount of red pepper flakes.

Enjoy your delicious and simple Spaghetti Aglio e Olio!

Margherita Pizza

Ingredients

- **250g** pizza dough
- **200g** canned San Marzano tomatoes, crushed
- **200g** fresh mozzarella, sliced
- **Fresh basil leaves**
- **2 tbsp** extra virgin olive oil
- **Salt**, to taste

Instructions

1. **Preheat Oven**: Preheat your oven to the highest setting (around 475°F/245°C) with a pizza stone if available.
2. **Prepare the Dough**: Roll out the pizza dough on a floured surface to your desired thickness.
3. **Add Toppings**: Spread crushed tomatoes over the dough, leaving a small border. Add mozzarella slices and season with salt.
4. **Bake**: Transfer the pizza to the oven and bake for 10-15 minutes until the crust is golden and cheese is bubbly.
5. **Finish**: Remove from the oven, drizzle with olive oil, and top with fresh basil before slicing.

Lasagna

Ingredients

- **9-12 lasagna noodles**
- **500g** ground beef or Italian sausage
- **400g** marinara sauce
- **500g** ricotta cheese
- **2 cups** shredded mozzarella cheese
- **1 cup** grated Parmesan cheese
- **1 egg**
- **Salt and pepper**, to taste
- **Fresh basil** (optional)

Instructions

1. **Cook Noodles**: Cook lasagna noodles according to package instructions. Drain and set aside.
2. **Make Filling**: In a skillet, brown the ground meat. Add marinara sauce and simmer for a few minutes. In a bowl, mix ricotta, egg, salt, and pepper.
3. **Layer**: In a baking dish, spread a layer of meat sauce, followed by noodles, ricotta mixture, and mozzarella. Repeat layers, finishing with sauce and mozzarella on top.
4. **Bake**: Preheat the oven to 375°F (190°C) and bake for 30-40 minutes until golden and bubbly. Let it rest before serving.

Risotto alla Milanese

Ingredients

- **1 cup** Arborio rice
- **4 cups** chicken or vegetable broth
- **1 small onion**, finely chopped
- **2 tbsp** butter
- **2 tbsp** olive oil
- **½ cup** dry white wine
- **¼ tsp** saffron threads
- **½ cup** grated Parmesan cheese
- **Salt and pepper**, to taste

Instructions

1. **Heat Broth**: In a saucepan, warm the broth and add saffron to infuse flavor.
2. **Sauté Onion**: In a large skillet, heat butter and olive oil. Add chopped onion and sauté until translucent.
3. **Toast Rice**: Add Arborio rice, stirring for about 2 minutes until slightly translucent.
4. **Add Wine**: Pour in white wine and stir until absorbed.
5. **Cook Risotto**: Gradually add warm broth, one ladle at a time, stirring frequently until absorbed. Continue until the rice is creamy and al dente.
6. **Finish**: Stir in Parmesan cheese, season with salt and pepper, and serve hot.

Enjoy your cooking!

Caprese Salad

Ingredients

- **3 large tomatoes**, sliced
- **250g** fresh mozzarella, sliced
- **Fresh basil leaves**
- **2 tbsp** extra virgin olive oil
- **Salt and pepper**, to taste

Instructions

1. **Layer Ingredients**: Arrange alternating slices of tomato and mozzarella on a plate.
2. **Season**: Tuck fresh basil leaves between the layers.
3. **Drizzle**: Drizzle with olive oil and season with salt and pepper before serving.

Osso Buco

Ingredients

- **4 veal shanks**
- **2 tbsp** olive oil
- **1 onion**, chopped
- **2 carrots**, chopped
- **2 celery stalks**, chopped
- **2 garlic cloves**, minced
- **1 cup** dry white wine
- **2 cups** beef broth
- **1 can (400g)** diced tomatoes
- **Salt and pepper**, to taste
- **Fresh parsley**, for garnish

Instructions

1. **Sear Shanks**: Heat olive oil in a pot and brown veal shanks on all sides. Remove and set aside.
2. **Sauté Vegetables**: Add onion, carrots, celery, and garlic. Cook until softened.
3. **Add Liquids**: Return shanks to the pot. Add wine, broth, and tomatoes. Season with salt and pepper.
4. **Simmer**: Cover and simmer for 1.5 to 2 hours until meat is tender. Garnish with parsley before serving.

Fettuccine Alfredo

Ingredients

- **400g** fettuccine
- **1 cup** heavy cream
- **½ cup** unsalted butter
- **1 cup** grated Parmesan cheese
- **Salt and pepper**, to taste
- **Chopped parsley**, for garnish (optional)

Instructions

1. **Cook Pasta**: Boil fettuccine according to package instructions. Drain, reserving some pasta water.
2. **Make Sauce**: In a pan, melt butter over medium heat. Add cream and bring to a simmer.
3. **Combine**: Stir in Parmesan until melted. Add pasta and toss. If too thick, add reserved pasta water.
4. **Season**: Season with salt and pepper. Garnish with parsley if desired.

Bruschetta al Pomodoro

Ingredients

- **1 baguette**, sliced
- **4 large tomatoes**, diced
- **2 cloves** garlic, minced
- **¼ cup** fresh basil, chopped
- **2 tbsp** extra virgin olive oil
- **Salt and pepper**, to taste

Instructions

1. **Toast Bread**: Toast baguette slices until golden.
2. **Mix Topping**: In a bowl, combine tomatoes, garlic, basil, olive oil, salt, and pepper.
3. **Top Bread**: Spoon the tomato mixture onto toasted bread and serve immediately.

Tiramisu

Ingredients

- **250g** mascarpone cheese
- **3 eggs**, separated
- **100g** sugar
- **1 cup** brewed espresso, cooled
- **24 ladyfingers**
- **Cocoa powder**, for dusting

Instructions

1. **Prepare Cream**: Whisk egg yolks with sugar until pale. Fold in mascarpone.
2. **Whip Egg Whites**: Beat egg whites until stiff peaks form and gently fold into mascarpone mixture.
3. **Layer**: Dip ladyfingers in espresso, layer in a dish, and spread mascarpone mixture on top. Repeat layers.
4. **Chill**: Refrigerate for at least 4 hours. Dust with cocoa powder before serving.

Pesto Genovese

Ingredients

- **2 cups** fresh basil leaves
- **¼ cup** pine nuts
- **½ cup** grated Parmesan cheese
- **2 cloves** garlic
- **½ cup** extra virgin olive oil
- **Salt**, to taste

Instructions

1. **Blend Ingredients**: In a food processor, combine basil, pine nuts, Parmesan, and garlic. Pulse until finely chopped.
2. **Add Oil**: With the processor running, slowly drizzle in olive oil until smooth. Season with salt.

Carbonara

Ingredients

- **400g** spaghetti
- **150g** pancetta or guanciale, diced
- **3 large eggs**
- **1 cup** grated Parmesan cheese
- **Salt and pepper**, to taste
- **Chopped parsley**, for garnish (optional)

Instructions

1. **Cook Pasta**: Boil spaghetti until al dente. Reserve some pasta water.
2. **Cook Meat**: In a pan, cook pancetta until crispy.
3. **Mix Eggs**: In a bowl, whisk eggs with cheese, salt, and pepper.
4. **Combine**: Drain pasta, add to pancetta, and remove from heat. Quickly stir in egg mixture, adding reserved pasta water as needed.
5. **Serve**: Garnish with parsley if desired.

Pollo alla Cacciatora

Ingredients

- **4 chicken thighs**
- **2 tbsp** olive oil
- **1 onion**, sliced
- **2 garlic cloves**, minced
- **2 bell peppers**, sliced
- **400g** canned tomatoes
- **1 cup** chicken broth
- **Salt and pepper**, to taste
- **Fresh herbs**, for garnish

Instructions

1. **Brown Chicken**: Heat olive oil in a pan. Brown chicken thighs on both sides. Remove and set aside.
2. **Sauté Vegetables**: In the same pan, add onion, garlic, and bell peppers. Cook until softened.
3. **Add Liquids**: Return chicken to the pan. Add tomatoes and broth. Season with salt and pepper.
4. **Simmer**: Cover and simmer for 30-40 minutes until chicken is cooked through. Garnish with fresh herbs before serving.

Enjoy your cooking!

Gnocchi di Patate

Ingredients

- **1 kg** potatoes (preferably starchy)
- **250g** all-purpose flour (plus extra for dusting)
- **1 egg**
- **Salt**, to taste

Instructions

1. **Cook Potatoes**: Boil potatoes until tender. Peel while hot and mash until smooth.
2. **Make Dough**: Combine mashed potatoes, flour, egg, and salt. Knead gently until a smooth dough forms.
3. **Shape Gnocchi**: Divide dough into sections, roll into ropes, and cut into small pieces. Use a fork to create ridges.
4. **Cook Gnocchi**: Boil a pot of salted water. Add gnocchi; they are done when they float to the surface. Drain and serve with your favorite sauce.

Bolognese Sauce

Ingredients

- **500g** ground beef or a mix of beef and pork
- **1 onion**, finely chopped
- **1 carrot**, finely chopped
- **1 celery stalk**, finely chopped
- **2 cloves** garlic, minced
- **400g** canned tomatoes, crushed
- **½ cup** red wine
- **Salt and pepper**, to taste
- **Fresh basil** (optional)

Instructions

1. **Sauté Vegetables**: In a large pan, heat olive oil. Add onion, carrot, celery, and garlic. Sauté until softened.
2. **Brown Meat**: Add ground meat and cook until browned.
3. **Add Liquids**: Stir in red wine and cook for a few minutes. Add crushed tomatoes, salt, and pepper.
4. **Simmer**: Reduce heat and simmer for at least 30 minutes, stirring occasionally. Finish with fresh basil if desired.

Eggplant Parmesan

Ingredients

- **2 large eggplants**, sliced
- **2 cups** marinara sauce
- **2 cups** shredded mozzarella cheese
- **1 cup** grated Parmesan cheese
- **1 cup** all-purpose flour
- **2 eggs**, beaten
- **2 cups** breadcrumbs
- **Salt and pepper**, to taste
- **Fresh basil**, for garnish

Instructions

1. **Prepare Eggplant**: Sprinkle salt on eggplant slices and let sit for 30 minutes to draw out moisture. Rinse and pat dry.
2. **Bread Eggplant**: Dredge slices in flour, dip in beaten eggs, and coat with breadcrumbs.
3. **Fry**: Fry in olive oil until golden brown. Drain on paper towels.
4. **Layer**: In a baking dish, layer marinara sauce, eggplant, mozzarella, and Parmesan. Repeat layers and finish with cheese.
5. **Bake**: Bake at 375°F (190°C) for 30-40 minutes until bubbly and golden. Garnish with basil before serving.

Zuppa Toscana

Ingredients

- **1 lb** Italian sausage, casings removed
- **4 cups** chicken broth
- **2 cups** kale, chopped
- **3 potatoes**, diced
- **1 onion**, chopped
- **2 cloves** garlic, minced
- **½ cup** heavy cream
- **Salt and pepper**, to taste

Instructions

1. **Cook Sausage**: In a pot, brown the sausage over medium heat. Remove and set aside.
2. **Sauté Vegetables**: In the same pot, add onion and garlic. Sauté until translucent.
3. **Add Broth and Potatoes**: Add chicken broth and diced potatoes. Simmer until potatoes are tender.
4. **Add Kale and Cream**: Stir in kale and heavy cream. Return sausage to the pot. Season with salt and pepper. Simmer for a few more minutes before serving.

Cannoli

Ingredients

- **250g** ricotta cheese
- **100g** powdered sugar
- **½ tsp** vanilla extract
- **20** cannoli shells
- **Chocolate chips** or chopped pistachios for filling
- **Cocoa powder** for dusting

Instructions

1. **Prepare Filling**: In a bowl, mix ricotta, powdered sugar, and vanilla until smooth. Fold in chocolate chips or pistachios.
2. **Fill Shells**: Using a pastry bag, fill the cannoli shells with the ricotta mixture.
3. **Serve**: Dust with cocoa powder before serving.

Pasta Primavera

Ingredients

- **400g** pasta (your choice)
- **2 cups** mixed vegetables (bell peppers, zucchini, carrots, etc.)
- **2 cloves** garlic, minced
- **¼ cup** olive oil
- **½ cup** grated Parmesan cheese
- **Salt and pepper**, to taste
- **Fresh basil**, for garnish

Instructions

1. **Cook Pasta**: Boil pasta according to package instructions. Drain and set aside.
2. **Sauté Vegetables**: In a large pan, heat olive oil. Add garlic and mixed vegetables. Sauté until tender.
3. **Combine**: Add cooked pasta to the pan, toss to combine, and season with salt and pepper.
4. **Finish**: Stir in Parmesan and garnish with fresh basil before serving.

Stuffed Peppers

Ingredients

- **4 bell peppers**, halved and seeds removed
- **300g** ground meat (beef, turkey, or sausage)
- **1 cup** cooked rice
- **1 onion**, chopped
- **1 can (400g)** diced tomatoes
- **1 tsp** Italian seasoning
- **Salt and pepper**, to taste
- **1 cup** shredded cheese (optional)

Instructions

1. **Preheat Oven**: Preheat oven to 375°F (190°C).
2. **Cook Filling**: In a skillet, sauté onion until translucent. Add ground meat and cook until browned. Stir in rice, tomatoes, Italian seasoning, salt, and pepper.
3. **Stuff Peppers**: Fill pepper halves with the meat mixture and place in a baking dish. Top with cheese if desired.
4. **Bake**: Cover with foil and bake for 30 minutes. Remove foil and bake for an additional 10-15 minutes until peppers are tender.

Frittata

Ingredients

- **6 large eggs**
- **1 cup** mixed vegetables (spinach, bell peppers, onions, etc.)
- **½ cup** cheese (feta, mozzarella, or cheddar)
- **Salt and pepper**, to taste
- **2 tbsp** olive oil

Instructions

1. **Preheat Oven**: Preheat your oven to 375°F (190°C).
2. **Sauté Vegetables**: In an oven-safe skillet, heat olive oil. Add mixed vegetables and sauté until tender.
3. **Whisk Eggs**: In a bowl, whisk eggs with salt and pepper. Pour over the vegetables in the skillet.
4. **Add Cheese**: Sprinkle cheese on top. Cook on the stove for a few minutes until edges set.
5. **Bake**: Transfer to the oven and bake for 15-20 minutes until the frittata is set. Slice and serve warm.

Enjoy your cooking!

Shrimp Scampi

Ingredients

- **500g** shrimp, peeled and deveined
- **4 cloves** garlic, minced
- **½ cup** white wine
- **¼ cup** lemon juice
- **¼ cup** butter
- **2 tbsp** olive oil
- **Salt and pepper**, to taste
- **Chopped parsley**, for garnish
- **Cooked pasta**, for serving

Instructions

1. **Sauté Shrimp**: In a large skillet, heat olive oil and butter over medium heat. Add garlic and sauté until fragrant, then add shrimp.
2. **Add Liquids**: Cook shrimp until pink, then add white wine and lemon juice. Simmer for a few minutes.
3. **Season**: Season with salt and pepper. Toss with cooked pasta and garnish with parsley before serving.

Arancini

Ingredients

- **2 cups** risotto (cooked and cooled)
- **100g** mozzarella cheese, cubed
- **1 cup** breadcrumbs
- **2 eggs**, beaten
- **Flour**, for dusting
- **Oil**, for frying

Instructions

1. **Form Balls**: Take a small amount of risotto and flatten it in your hand. Place a cube of mozzarella in the center and mold the risotto around it to form a ball.
2. **Coat**: Dredge the balls in flour, dip in beaten eggs, and coat with breadcrumbs.
3. **Fry**: Heat oil in a deep pan. Fry the arancini until golden brown. Drain on paper towels before serving.

Minestrone Soup

Ingredients

- **1 onion**, chopped
- **2 carrots**, diced
- **2 celery stalks**, diced
- **2 cloves** garlic, minced
- **400g** canned diced tomatoes
- **4 cups** vegetable or chicken broth
- **2 cups** mixed vegetables (zucchini, green beans, etc.)
- **1 can (400g)** cannellini beans, drained
- **Salt and pepper**, to taste
- **Fresh basil**, for garnish

Instructions

1. **Sauté Vegetables**: In a large pot, heat olive oil. Add onion, carrots, and celery. Sauté until softened. Add garlic and cook briefly.
2. **Add Liquids**: Stir in tomatoes, broth, and mixed vegetables. Bring to a boil.
3. **Simmer**: Add cannellini beans and simmer for 20-30 minutes. Season with salt and pepper. Garnish with fresh basil before serving.

Vitello Tonnato

Ingredients

- **500g** veal roast
- **1 cup** vegetable broth
- **1 can (200g)** tuna in oil, drained
- **2 anchovy fillets**
- **½ cup** mayonnaise
- **2 tbsp** capers
- **Juice of 1 lemon**
- **Salt and pepper**, to taste

Instructions

1. **Cook Veal**: Sear veal in a pan, then add broth. Cover and simmer until tender. Let cool before slicing.
2. **Make Sauce**: In a blender, combine tuna, anchovies, mayonnaise, capers, lemon juice, salt, and pepper. Blend until smooth.
3. **Serve**: Arrange veal slices on a platter and top with the tuna sauce.

Panna Cotta

Ingredients

- **2 cups** heavy cream
- **½ cup** sugar
- **1 tsp** vanilla extract
- **2 ½ tsp** gelatin
- **3 tbsp** cold water

Instructions

1. **Bloom Gelatin**: In a small bowl, sprinkle gelatin over cold water and let sit for 5 minutes.
2. **Heat Cream**: In a saucepan, heat cream, sugar, and vanilla until sugar dissolves. Remove from heat and stir in gelatin until dissolved.
3. **Chill**: Pour into molds and refrigerate for at least 4 hours until set. Serve with fruit or sauce.

Garlic Bread

Ingredients

- **1 baguette**
- **100g** butter, softened
- **4 cloves** garlic, minced
- **2 tbsp** parsley, chopped
- **Salt**, to taste

Instructions

1. **Preheat Oven**: Preheat oven to 375°F (190°C).
2. **Make Garlic Butter**: In a bowl, mix softened butter, garlic, parsley, and salt.
3. **Spread and Bake**: Slice the baguette and spread garlic butter on each piece. Bake for 10-15 minutes until golden.

Ribollita

Ingredients

- **1 onion**, chopped
- **2 carrots**, diced
- **2 celery stalks**, diced
- **2 cloves** garlic, minced
- **1 can (400g)** diced tomatoes
- **4 cups** vegetable broth
- **2 cups** kale, chopped
- **1 can (400g)** cannellini beans, drained
- **Salt and pepper**, to taste
- **Stale bread**, for serving

Instructions

1. **Sauté Vegetables**: In a large pot, heat olive oil. Add onion, carrots, and celery. Sauté until softened, then add garlic.
2. **Add Liquids**: Stir in tomatoes, broth, kale, and cannellini beans. Simmer for 30 minutes.
3. **Serve**: Serve hot over pieces of stale bread, seasoning with salt and pepper.

Spaghetti Carbonara

Ingredients

- **400g** spaghetti
- **150g** pancetta or guanciale, diced
- **3 large eggs**
- **1 cup** grated Parmesan cheese
- **Salt and pepper**, to taste
- **Chopped parsley**, for garnish (optional)

Instructions

1. **Cook Pasta**: Boil spaghetti until al dente. Reserve some pasta water.
2. **Cook Meat**: In a pan, cook pancetta until crispy.
3. **Mix Eggs**: In a bowl, whisk eggs with cheese, salt, and pepper.
4. **Combine**: Drain pasta, add to pancetta, and remove from heat. Quickly stir in egg mixture, adding reserved pasta water as needed.
5. **Serve**: Garnish with parsley if desired.

Enjoy your cooking!

Saltimbocca

Ingredients

- **4 veal cutlets**
- **8 slices** prosciutto
- **8 fresh sage leaves**
- **½ cup** white wine
- **2 tbsp** olive oil
- **Salt and pepper**, to taste

Instructions

1. **Prepare Cutlets**: Place a slice of prosciutto and a sage leaf on each cutlet, securing with a toothpick.
2. **Sear**: Heat olive oil in a pan. Cook cutlets for 2-3 minutes on each side until golden.
3. **Add Wine**: Pour in white wine and simmer until reduced. Season with salt and pepper before serving.

Crostini with Tapenade

Ingredients

- **1 baguette**, sliced
- **1 cup** black olives, pitted
- **2 tbsp** capers
- **2 cloves** garlic
- **2 tbsp** olive oil
- **Fresh herbs (optional)**

Instructions

1. **Prepare Tapenade**: In a food processor, combine olives, capers, garlic, and olive oil. Blend until smooth.
2. **Toast Bread**: Toast baguette slices until golden.
3. **Spread and Serve**: Top toasted bread with tapenade and garnish with fresh herbs if desired.

Torta della Nonna

Ingredients

- **1 package** shortcrust pastry
- **500g** ricotta cheese
- **100g** sugar
- **2 eggs**
- **1 tsp** vanilla extract
- **Pine nuts**, for topping
- **Powdered sugar**, for dusting

Instructions

1. **Preheat Oven**: Preheat to 350°F (175°C).
2. **Make Filling**: In a bowl, mix ricotta, sugar, eggs, and vanilla until smooth.
3. **Assemble**: Line a pie dish with pastry, fill with ricotta mixture, and top with pine nuts.
4. **Bake**: Bake for 30-35 minutes until set. Cool and dust with powdered sugar before serving.

Sicilian Caponata

Ingredients

- **1 eggplant**, diced
- **2 celery stalks**, diced
- **1 onion**, chopped
- **400g** canned tomatoes, diced
- **¼ cup** capers
- **¼ cup** olives, pitted and chopped
- **2 tbsp** red wine vinegar
- **2 tbsp** olive oil
- **Salt and pepper**, to taste

Instructions

1. **Sauté Vegetables**: In a large pan, heat olive oil. Add eggplant, onion, and celery, cooking until softened.
2. **Add Tomatoes**: Stir in canned tomatoes, capers, olives, and vinegar. Simmer for 20-30 minutes.
3. **Season**: Season with salt and pepper before serving warm or at room temperature.

Stuffed Zucchini

Ingredients

- **4 zucchini**, halved and scooped
- **300g** ground meat (beef or turkey)
- **1 onion**, chopped
- **1 cup** breadcrumbs
- **½ cup** grated Parmesan cheese
- **1 can (400g)** diced tomatoes
- **Salt and pepper**, to taste

Instructions

1. **Preheat Oven**: Preheat to 375°F (190°C).
2. **Cook Filling**: In a skillet, sauté onion until soft. Add ground meat and cook through. Stir in breadcrumbs, Parmesan, and diced tomatoes. Season with salt and pepper.
3. **Stuff Zucchini**: Fill zucchini halves with the meat mixture and place in a baking dish.
4. **Bake**: Bake for 25-30 minutes until zucchini is tender.

Pasta e Fagioli

Ingredients

- **200g** pasta (small shapes)
- **1 can (400g)** cannellini beans, drained
- **1 onion**, chopped
- **2 carrots**, diced
- **2 celery stalks**, diced
- **4 cups** vegetable or chicken broth
- **Salt and pepper**, to taste
- **Fresh parsley**, for garnish

Instructions

1. **Sauté Vegetables**: In a pot, heat olive oil. Add onion, carrots, and celery. Sauté until softened.
2. **Add Broth**: Pour in broth and bring to a boil. Add pasta and cook according to package instructions.
3. **Add Beans**: Stir in cannellini beans. Season with salt and pepper. Garnish with fresh parsley before serving.

Chocolate Soufflé

Ingredients

- **100g** dark chocolate, chopped
- **3 eggs**, separated
- **50g** sugar
- **2 tbsp** butter (for greasing)
- **Powdered sugar**, for dusting

Instructions

1. **Preheat Oven**: Preheat to 375°F (190°C). Grease ramekins with butter.
2. **Melt Chocolate**: Melt chocolate in a bowl over simmering water. Let cool slightly.
3. **Whisk Egg Yolks**: In a bowl, whisk egg yolks with sugar until pale. Stir in melted chocolate.
4. **Whip Egg Whites**: In another bowl, whip egg whites until stiff peaks form. Gently fold into chocolate mixture.
5. **Bake**: Divide into ramekins and bake for 12-15 minutes. Dust with powdered sugar before serving.

Farro Salad

Ingredients

- **1 cup** farro
- **2 cups** water or broth
- **1 cucumber**, diced
- **1 bell pepper**, diced
- **¼ cup** red onion, chopped
- **¼ cup** parsley, chopped
- **¼ cup** olive oil
- **Juice of 1 lemon**
- **Salt and pepper**, to taste

Instructions

1. **Cook Farro**: Rinse farro and combine with water or broth in a pot. Bring to a boil, then reduce heat and simmer for 25-30 minutes until tender. Drain.
2. **Mix Salad**: In a large bowl, combine cooked farro, cucumber, bell pepper, onion, and parsley.
3. **Dress**: Drizzle with olive oil and lemon juice. Season with salt and pepper before serving.

Enjoy your cooking!

Grilled Octopus

Ingredients

- **1 kg** octopus, cleaned
- **¼ cup** olive oil
- **2 cloves** garlic, minced
- **Juice of 1 lemon**
- **Salt and pepper**, to taste
- **Fresh parsley**, for garnish

Instructions

1. **Cook Octopus**: Boil octopus in salted water for about 45 minutes until tender. Drain and let cool.
2. **Marinate**: In a bowl, mix olive oil, garlic, lemon juice, salt, and pepper. Add octopus and marinate for at least 30 minutes.
3. **Grill**: Preheat grill and cook octopus for 3-4 minutes per side until charred. Garnish with parsley before serving.

Ricotta Cheesecake

Ingredients

- **500g** ricotta cheese
- **200g** sugar
- **3 eggs**
- **1 tsp** vanilla extract
- **1 tbsp** lemon zest
- **1 cup** crushed graham crackers
- **50g** melted butter

Instructions

1. **Preheat Oven**: Preheat to 350°F (175°C).
2. **Prepare Crust**: Mix crushed graham crackers with melted butter. Press into the bottom of a springform pan.
3. **Mix Filling**: In a bowl, blend ricotta, sugar, eggs, vanilla, and lemon zest until smooth.
4. **Bake**: Pour filling over the crust and bake for 45-50 minutes until set. Cool before serving.

Fagottini di Pasta

Ingredients

- **250g** fresh pasta sheets
- **300g** ricotta cheese
- **100g** spinach, cooked and chopped
- **50g** grated Parmesan cheese
- **Salt and pepper**, to taste
- **Tomato sauce**, for serving

Instructions

1. **Prepare Filling**: In a bowl, mix ricotta, spinach, Parmesan, salt, and pepper.
2. **Fill Pasta**: Cut pasta sheets into squares, place a spoonful of filling in the center, and fold to form triangles, sealing edges.
3. **Cook**: Boil in salted water for 3-4 minutes. Serve with tomato sauce.

Insalata di Mare

Ingredients

- **500g** mixed seafood (shrimp, calamari, mussels)
- **2 cloves** garlic, minced
- **¼ cup** olive oil
- **Juice of 1 lemon**
- **Salt and pepper**, to taste
- **Fresh parsley**, chopped

Instructions

1. **Cook Seafood**: Boil or steam seafood until cooked through. Drain and cool.
2. **Dress Salad**: In a bowl, combine olive oil, garlic, lemon juice, salt, and pepper. Toss with seafood.
3. **Serve**: Garnish with fresh parsley before serving.

Polenta with Mushrooms

Ingredients

- **1 cup** polenta
- **4 cups** water or broth
- **300g** mushrooms, sliced
- **2 cloves** garlic, minced
- **¼ cup** grated Parmesan cheese
- **Salt and pepper**, to taste
- **Olive oil**, for cooking

Instructions

1. **Cook Polenta**: Bring water or broth to a boil. Gradually whisk in polenta and cook until thickened, about 20-30 minutes. Stir in Parmesan.
2. **Sauté Mushrooms**: In a pan, heat olive oil, add garlic and mushrooms, and sauté until tender. Season with salt and pepper.
3. **Serve**: Spoon polenta onto plates and top with mushrooms.

Frittelle di Mele

Ingredients

- **2 apples**, peeled and sliced
- **1 cup** flour
- **2 tbsp** sugar
- **1 tsp** baking powder
- **1 egg**
- **½ cup** milk
- **Oil**, for frying
- **Powdered sugar**, for dusting

Instructions

1. **Prepare Batter**: In a bowl, mix flour, sugar, baking powder, egg, and milk until smooth.
2. **Coat Apples**: Dip apple slices in the batter.
3. **Fry**: Heat oil in a pan and fry apple slices until golden. Drain on paper towels and dust with powdered sugar.

Tagliatelle al Tartufo

Ingredients

- **400g** tagliatelle
- **50g** truffle butter
- **¼ cup** grated Parmesan cheese
- **Salt and pepper**, to taste
- **Fresh truffle** (optional), for garnish

Instructions

1. **Cook Pasta**: Boil tagliatelle until al dente. Drain, reserving some pasta water.
2. **Mix with Butter**: In a pan, melt truffle butter and add pasta. Toss to combine, adding reserved water if needed.
3. **Serve**: Top with Parmesan and garnish with shaved truffle if desired.

Zucchini Noodles with Pesto

Ingredients

- **2 large zucchinis**, spiralized
- **1 cup** basil pesto
- **½ cup** cherry tomatoes, halved
- **Salt and pepper**, to taste
- **Parmesan cheese**, for serving

Instructions

1. **Sauté Zucchini**: In a pan, lightly sauté zucchini noodles for 2-3 minutes until just tender.
2. **Add Pesto**: Remove from heat and toss with pesto and cherry tomatoes.
3. **Serve**: Season with salt and pepper, and top with Parmesan cheese before serving.

Enjoy your cooking!

Prosciutto e Melone

Ingredients

- **200g** prosciutto, thinly sliced
- **1 ripe cantaloupe or honeydew melon**, sliced

Instructions

1. **Prepare Melon**: Cut the melon into wedges or cubes.
2. **Serve**: Arrange prosciutto on a platter and wrap around melon slices. Serve chilled as an appetizer.

Sgombro Marinato

Ingredients

- **2 mackerel fillets**
- **½ cup** olive oil
- **¼ cup** white vinegar
- **2 cloves** garlic, minced
- **Salt and pepper**, to taste
- **Fresh herbs (parsley or dill)**, for garnish

Instructions

1. **Marinate Fish**: In a bowl, mix olive oil, vinegar, garlic, salt, and pepper. Add mackerel fillets and marinate for at least 1 hour in the refrigerator.
2. **Serve**: Arrange on a plate and garnish with fresh herbs.

Crespelle alla Fiorentina

Ingredients

- **250g** flour
- **4 eggs**
- **500ml** milk
- **400g** ricotta cheese
- **200g** spinach, cooked and chopped
- **100g** grated Parmesan cheese
- **Tomato sauce**, for serving

Instructions

1. **Make Batter**: Whisk together flour, eggs, and milk until smooth. Let rest for 30 minutes.
2. **Cook Crespelle**: In a non-stick skillet, pour a ladle of batter and cook until golden on both sides. Repeat until batter is finished.
3. **Prepare Filling**: Mix ricotta, spinach, and half the Parmesan in a bowl.
4. **Assemble**: Fill each crespella with the ricotta mixture, roll up, and place in a baking dish. Top with tomato sauce and remaining Parmesan.
5. **Bake**: Bake at 375°F (190°C) for 20 minutes until heated through.

Baked Ziti

Ingredients

- **400g** ziti pasta
- **500g** ricotta cheese
- **400g** marinara sauce
- **200g** mozzarella cheese, shredded
- **100g** grated Parmesan cheese
- **Salt and pepper**, to taste

Instructions

1. **Cook Pasta**: Boil ziti until al dente. Drain and set aside.
2. **Mix Ingredients**: In a bowl, combine cooked ziti, ricotta, marinara sauce, half of the mozzarella, salt, and pepper.
3. **Assemble**: Spread half the mixture in a baking dish. Top with remaining mixture and sprinkle with mozzarella and Parmesan.
4. **Bake**: Bake at 375°F (190°C) for 25-30 minutes until bubbly and golden.

Limoncello Torte

Ingredients

- **200g** digestive biscuits, crushed
- **100g** butter, melted
- **400g** mascarpone cheese
- **200ml** limoncello
- **100g** sugar
- **Juice of 2 lemons**
- **2 eggs**

Instructions

1. **Prepare Crust**: Mix crushed biscuits with melted butter and press into the bottom of a springform pan.
2. **Make Filling**: In a bowl, whisk together mascarpone, limoncello, sugar, lemon juice, and eggs until smooth.
3. **Bake**: Pour filling over the crust and bake at 350°F (175°C) for 30-35 minutes. Cool and refrigerate before serving.

Affogato

Ingredients

- **2 scoops** vanilla gelato or ice cream
- **1 shot** hot espresso
- **Chocolate shavings** or cocoa powder, for garnish

Instructions

1. **Prepare**: Place scoops of gelato in a serving glass.
2. **Add Espresso**: Pour hot espresso over the gelato.
3. **Garnish and Serve**: Top with chocolate shavings or a dusting of cocoa powder.

Enjoy your cooking!

9 798330 438815